Contents

Introduction

Bandanas are both practical and useful. Long associated with cowboys in the Wild West, the basic size and design of the bandana has altered little over the centuries. The traditional style of paisley borders, illustrations and spots are instantly familiar, nostalgic and festive.

Here are 11 original projects for your home and garden created with this timeless icon. Available in an array of colours and patterns, bandanas make a striking design statement when upcycled into these eye-catching and practical makes.

Each project has clear instructions and colour photographs to help you achieve perfect results. If you're new to sewing, don't worry: there's a handy techniques section that explains all the basic skills needed.

Shopping-bag tidy

This is a neat little set of detachable pockets to keep essentials from disappearing into the depths of your bag. Attach this to the handles of your market basket and avoid scrabbling through your groceries for your keys or phone.

1 Cut two rectangles from the bandana: 10 x 8in (25 x 20cm) and 10 x 7in (25 x 18cm). Using an iron, fuse the cotton wadding to the wrong side of the smaller piece of bandana fabric with the fusible interfacing. Fuse the heavyweight fabric stiffener to the wrong side of the larger piece of bandana fabric, starting ⅜in (1cm) below the top edge.

2 To make the back piece: lay the larger piece of bandana fabric down right side up in front of you and with the ⅜in (1cm) unstiffened edge furthest from you. Cut the elastic into two equal lengths and fold them in half. Pin each loop in position along the top edge, 2½in (6cm) from either end, with their raw edges just protruding over the top edge of the fabric.

SUPPLIES

- One bandana measuring 18in (46cm) square, or fabric of your choice cut to those measurements
- 10 x 7in (25 x 18cm) of cotton wadding
- 10 x 7in (25 x 18cm) of fusible interfacing
- 10 x 7½in (25 x 19cm) of heavyweight iron-on fabric stiffener
- 10½ x 12in (27 x 30cm) of linen for backing and binding
- Two self-cover buttons ¾in (2cm) in diameter
- 24in (60cm) of ⅛in (3mm)-wide cord elastic
- Two small buttons
- Scissors
- Iron
- Sewing needles and pins
- White cotton thread
- Thread to match the base colour of your bandana
- Sewing machine

TIP
You could use up scraps from other projects to make this. Cut paper patterns first to all the correct dimensions to work out if you have large enough pieces to use.

TIP
This project can be made to many different dimensions; just adapt it to suit your needs. Different-sized pockets, and even a little zipped purse, could be incorporated.

3 Lay the lining fabric on top, covering the elastic loops, aligning all edges and pinning or tacking along the top edge.

4 Stitch a ⅜in (1cm) seam along the top edge, sewing through the two layers of fabric just outside the edge of the stiffener. Stitch back and forth as you pass over the ends of the elastic for extra strength. Open out and press the seam towards the bandana fabric, avoiding ironing the cord elastic.

5 Fold the lining down behind, align all edges and press again. Pin or tack along all the sides and topstitch by machine ⅛in (3mm) in from the edges.

6 To make the pocket: fold the padded piece of bandana fabric in half, wrong sides together, so that it now measures 10 x 3½in (25 x 9cm) and tack along the folded edge.

7 Topstitch along the fold by machine ⅛in (3mm) from the edge. Lay it on top of the back piece, aligning the bottom and side edges. Pin or tack in position.

8 Mark two vertical lines from the bottom of the pocket to the top edge of the pocket, one 4¼in (10.5cm) from the right-hand edge and one 2½in (6cm) from the right-hand edge. Stitch the two lines by machine, reversing at the top edge for extra strength.

9 Cut a strip of linen 10 x 1⅜in (25 x 3.5cm). Lay it face down along the bottom of the pocket, with the raw edges aligning. Pin or tack in position before stitching a ¼in (5mm) seam using thread to match the colour of the linen.

10 Trim the selvedge down to make it even and fold the edge of the linen over twice to cover the raw edge of the seam and meet the stitch line on the back of your work. Pin or tack and hem by hand using overstitch.

11 Turn your work back over (bandana side up). Cut two more strips of linen, 8¾ x 1⅜in (22 x 3.5cm). Take one and pin it along the right-hand edge of your work, aligning the raw edges and leaving the ends to overhang by ⅜in (1cm) at the top and bottom. Pin or tack into position before stitching a ¼in (5mm) seam using thread to match the colour of the linen.

12 Trim the selvedge down to make it even and fold the edge of the linen over twice to cover the raw edge of the seam and meet the stitch line on the back of your work. Pin or tack and hem by hand using overstitch. As you do so, fold in ⅜in (1cm) at the top and bottom to cover any raw edges and make neat corners. Repeat this process with the other strip of linen along the left-hand edge.

13 Turn your work right side up. Stitch the two small buttons at the top of either vertical line of pocket stitching using thread to match the bandana.

14 Use scraps of your bandana fabric to cover the two self-cover buttons following the manufacturer's instructions. Stitch them into position, each one ¾in (2cm) below the two loops of elastic, as shown.

Notebook cover

This is a practical and reusable cover for a notebook or jotter.
The elastic strap marks a page or keeps your book closed and
your cuttings and receipts secure. It is a quick and easy
project that would make a great gift.

SUPPLIES

To cover one notebook 6 x 8¼ x ½in (15 x 21 x 1.25cm):

- One 18in (46cm) square bandana, or fabric of your choice cut to those measurements
- 18 x 10in (46 x 25cm) of iron-on interfacing
- 10in (25cm) of elastic to match the colour of the bandana
- Scissors
- Iron
- Sewing machine
- Sewing needles and pins
- White cotton thread
- Thread to match the colour of the bandana

1 Cut your bandana fabric to measure 18 x 10in (46 x 25cm). Fuse the iron-on interfacing to the wrong side of the bandana using an iron and following the manufacturer's instructions.

2 Zigzag stitch around all four edges of your fabric and finish off the thread ends. With the wrong side facing, fold the two long edges over by ⅜in (1cm) and stitch ¼in (5mm) from the zigzag edge to form a simple hem.

3 Wrap the fabric (wrong side out) around the notebook, tucking the vertical, short edges inside the front and back covers. This allows you to make sure the pattern lies evenly along the vertical opening edges of the covers; ease the fabric back and forth until you are happy with the lie of the pattern over the book's front, spine and back. Mark the fabric at the top and bottom of the opening edges with pins through both layers of fabric to ascertain the position for the seams of the flaps.

4 Slip the fabric off your notebook, retaining the pins in position. Fold back the right-hand flap enough to slip the length of elastic between the two layers of fabric and pin into position 2in (5cm) from the folded edge.

TIP
You can customize the size of your fabric notebook cover to fit different-sized notebooks. Cut the fabric to measure the same height as the notebook plus 1½in (4cm) and the same width as the measurement from the right-hand front edge of the front cover, around the spine, and to the left-hand edge of the back cover plus 6½in (16cm).

5 Stitch ¾in (2cm) seams along the top edge, starting at one corner, then stitching across the two fabric layers of the flap, along the single layer between the two flaps and finally across the two layers of the other flap. Repeat along the bottom edge. Trim the four corners, turn right side out and press with an iron, folding the top and bottom edges between the flaps down along the stitch line.

Knitting bag

The design of this useful bag was inspired by the memory of one my grandmother always carried with her. Pack away your knitting, with an extra ball or two of yarn, into a capacious, classic bag – perfect for travelling or just for tucking away under a cushion.

SUPPLIES

- Two bandanas, each at least 18in (46cm) square, or fabric of your choice cut to this measurement
- 18 x 36in (46 x 91.5cm) linen or cotton for lining
- Four small buttons
- Pair of 7in (18cm) wooden bag handles
- Scissors
- Needle and pins
- Threads to match the fabrics
- Sewing machine
- Iron
- Zipper foot

TIP

Using different proportions, you could make this into a cute little handbag instead.

1 Lay the two bandanas out, right sides together, and trim them if necessary, so that they are the same size. If you have any raw edges, zigzag stitch along them to reduce fraying. Pin or tack along the two sides and along the edge nearest to you – the unpinned edge furthest from you will be the top opening of your bag. Mark a point halfway down on both sides. Starting at one of these halfway points, stitch a ⅜in (1cm) seam by machine down to the bottom corner, along the bottom edge, and back up to the opposite halfway point, reverse stitching at either end. Remove the pins or tacking and trim the two bottom corners at a 90-degree angle, close to the stitch line. Press the seams open.

2 Fold the lining fabric in half, right sides together; the folded edge is the bottom of the lining. Pin or tack up the two sides so that the raw edges align. Mark a point on each side seam halfway up from the bottom edge minus ⅜in (1cm). Starting at these marks, stitch a ⅜in (1cm) seam down to the bottom folded edge, reverse stitching at either end. Remove the pins or tacking and trim the two bottom corners at a 45-degree angle close to the stitch line. Press the seams open.

3 Turn the lining right side out and place it inside the outer bandanas (which remain inside out). Align all the raw edges and the side seams, and pin or tack.

4 Mark a 6in (15cm) turning gap at the top centre of one side of the bag. Starting on one side of the turning gap, stitch a ⅜in (1cm) seam all the way around. Stop as you reach the point halfway along one side seam, working up to the stitching point from Step 2, and reverse stitch before breaking off. Start again on the other side of the halfway point, reverse stitching at the beginning, working all the way around to the halfway point on the other side, and reverse stitching again when you finish. Finally, work the last seam starting from the other side of the turning gap and working along and down to the halfway point. Remove the pins or tacking and trim the four top corners at a 90-degree angle close to the stitch line. Carefully ease the bag right side out through the turning gap.

5 Tease and manipulate the layers so that you have a good crisp edge all around the two sides of the top opening before pressing with a hot iron. Turn in the raw edges of the turning gap by ⅜in (1cm). Close the turning gap by hand with overstitch.

6 Place the bag down in front of you and turn the top edge down. Now fold the back top edge down by 2½in (6cm), pin and press.

7 Slip one of the wooden handles under the right-hand corner of the fold. First pin and then tack the fold back down into its previous position, making sure you stitch through all the layers of fabric.

8 Work methodically across the top of the bag, bunching the fabric you have already tacked to the right-hand side of the handle as you go, until the whole of the top edge is wrapped over the bottom of the handle. Using a zipper foot, machine stitch a hem ⅛in (3mm) in from the edge, and another ⅜in (1cm) below the bottom of the handle. These lines of sewing will be a bit fiddly; keep the fabric layers as flat as possible as they pass under the needle. Take it slowly, stopping if necessary, with the needle down, to raise the foot and rearrange the fabric.

9 Sew a pair of small buttons, one on the inside and one on the outside, just below the halfway mark on either side of the bag, centred on the side seams. Sandwich the fabric layers between them.

Card holder

This is a quick project, ideal for using up scraps of bandana, that would make a perfect gift. It is a practical wallet for holding loyalty cards, travel cards, bank cards and receipts. Make it in monochrome or use up contrasting vibrant scraps.

PREPARING THE PATTERN PIECES

From your bandana, cut:

Outer: 6¾ x 5in (17 x 13cm)

Inside: 6¾ x 5in (17 x 13cm)

Tall pocket: 6¾ x 7½in (17 x 19cm)

Short pocket: 6¾ x 5½in (17 x 14cm)

From your interfacing, cut:

Tall pocket: 6 x 6¾in (15 x 17cm)

Short pocket: 6 x 4¾in (15 x 12cm)

SUPPLIES

- One bandana, minimum dimensions 18in (46cm) square, or scraps of different colours – see left for dimensions needed
- 6 x 4½in (15 x 11.5cm) of heavyweight iron-on fabric stiffener
- 12in (30cm) square of iron-on interfacing
- 6in (15cm) of ¹⁄₁₆in (1mm)-wide cord elastic to match bandana
- Scissors
- Iron
- Sewing machine
- Sewing needle and pins
- Threads to match your bandana

1 Using an iron, fuse the heavyweight stiffener to the centre of the wrong side of your outer piece, leaving ⅜in (1cm) all the way around. Fuse the interfacing to the centre of the wrong side of each pocket piece, leaving ⅜in (1cm) all the way around.

2 Take the short pocket piece and fold it in half, wrong sides together, so that it now measures 6 x 2¾in (15 x 7cm) and press with an iron. Topstitch along the fold ⅛in (3mm) from the edge. Do the same with the tall pocket.

3 Lay the lining piece down in front of you right side up. Place the tall pocket piece on top of it so that the raw edges along the bottom align with the raw edges of the bottom of the lining piece. Pin or tack along the bottom edge.

4 Stitch a ¾in (2cm) seam along the bottom edge. Trim the seam to ¼in (5mm).

5 Place the short pocket piece over the tall pocket and lining pieces so that its top edge lies 1in (2.5cm) below the top edge of the tall pocket and pin in position.

6 Stitch along both side seams to hold the short pocket in position.

7 Lay your outer piece down right side up. Fold your cord elastic in half and position halfway down the left-hand edge so that its raw ends are projecting just beyond the edge and the loop is lying horizontally across the centre of the fabric.

TIP
Take care when using iron-on stiffener or interfacing: it is incredibly easy to place the wrong way down and make a mess of your iron. Identify which side has the adhesive on it: this can have a bobbly, raised appearance and a slight shininess from the glue. This side must always be face down and in contact with the wrong side of your fabric.

8 Place the lining and pocket pieces right side down on top of the outer piece, aligning all the raw edges. The lining piece will be ¾in (2cm) shorter than the short pocket and the outer pieces at the bottom edge. Pin or tack in position.

9 Sew a ⅜in (1cm) seam along both side edges and the top edge, then reverse stitch at the beginning and end for strength. Trim the seams down to ¼in (5mm). Clip the two top corners at 90 degrees.

10 Slip your hand through the open bottom edge, in between the tall and short pocket layers, and turn the work out through this gap. Tease the seams and prod the top two corners from inside to make them sharp before pressing your work with an iron. Pin or tack along the raw bottom edge.

TIP
With a little calculating, you can adjust the size and proportions of the card holder to store other everyday items such as travel passes and passports.

11 Stitch a ⅜in (1cm) hem along the bottom edge, reversing at each end. Clip the two bottom corners, then turn out through the short pocket opening, prodding the two bottom corners from inside the short pocket to make them sharp. Press with a hot iron (avoid ironing the elastic).

12 Topstitch just inside all four edges. 'Score' a vertical line up the centre of the pockets – I do this by running the tip of a small knitting needle, or a large tapestry needle, along the edge of a ruler. Stitch along the scored line by machine and finish off all thread ends carefully using a sewing needle.

TIP
You could use an elastic hairband to secure the card holder instead of the cord elastic.

Knitting-needle purse

This long purse can be used to store knitting needles. You could adapt the pattern to include pockets on the inside, or make a shorter purse to hold crochet hooks. I use a 6in (15cm)-deep version to carry a small sewing kit when I'm travelling.

1 Cut two pattern pieces (see template on page 19) from the bandana, lining fabric, wadding and the fusible interfacing. Fuse the wadding to the wrong sides of the bandana pieces using an iron and the fusible web. Place the two pieces of padded bandana right sides together, and pin or tack along the sides and bottom edges.

2 Sew a ½in (1.25cm) seam by machine, starting at one hinge-position mark (indicated on the pattern) and continuing around the outer edge until you reach the next mark, leaving the top section open. Reverse stitch at the start and finish to strengthen. Trim the two bottom corners at 45 degrees, making sure you don't snip the stitching.

SUPPLIES:
- One bandana, minimum dimensions 18in (46cm) square, or fabric of your choice cut to those measurements
- 18in (46cm) square of linen or cotton for lining
- 18in (46cm) square of cotton wadding
- 18in (46cm) square of fusible interfacing
- 5½in (14cm) glue-in purse frame
- Scissors
- Sewing needle and pins
- Sewing machine
- Threads to match the fabrics
- Iron
- Fabric glue

3 Press the seams open. Working on one of the bottom corners, create a box corner (see page 44) by putting your hand inside the lining and pushing the fabric out away from the seam. Align the side seam exactly with the bottom seam and press flat so that the corner forms a triangle. Sew across 1in (2.5cm) from the tip of the corner several times. Trim the seam to ⅛in (3mm). Repeat with the other bottom corner.

4 Place the two pieces of lining fabric right sides together and pin or tack around the side and bottom edges.

5 Stitch a ½in (1.25cm) seam from one hinge-position mark to the other (the long way), leaving a turning gap of 2¾in (7cm) along the bottom seam. Reverse stitch at the start and finish to strengthen.

6 Press the seams open and make box corners as you did at Step 3 for the bandana outer.

7 Cut notches at the hinge points marked on the pattern on both the outer and the lining pieces, just where the stitching starts and ends.

8 Turn the lining piece right side out, place it inside the outer bandana piece (still inside out) and align all the edges and the side seams carefully. Pin or tack around the top opening to hold the lining and outer piece in position before sewing.

9 Starting at the top centre of one side, stitch a ½in (1.25cm) seam all the way around the opening. Stop at the side seams with the needle down, raise the foot and manipulate your work under it so that you can continue without breaking the stitching. Clip small V-shapes near to but not through the seams along the top curves.

> ### TIP
> Make your own pattern to fit a purse frame. Draw a horizontal line and lay the frame on it so that the hinges are centred. Draw a line along the inside curve from one hinge to the other. Draw another pencil line ½in (1.25cm) outside the shape you have just drawn. This forms the top of the pattern. Draw 11½in (29cm) vertical lines extending down from the two hinge points, then a horizontal line at the bottom to join them.

10 Carefully ease the purse right side out through the turning gap in the lining. Slipstitch the turning gap closed by hand using overstitch.

11 With the lining pushed back inside the bandana outer, manipulate the layers so that you have a good crisp edge all around the top opening. Pin or tack it before topstitching ⅛in (3mm) in from the edge.

12 Run a line of fabric glue along the inside of one half of the frame, starting and stopping a few millimetres from the hinge at either side. Do the same along one side of the purse opening, starting and stopping ⅜in (1cm) from each side seam. Insert the fabric into the purse frame. Take care that the sides are at similar levels first, then feed the centre in. Use your fingers or a small crochet hook to push the fabric in snugly and to make sure that the line of topstitching is hidden within the frame. Leave to dry completely before gluing the other side.

TIP

If you want to make a firmer version of this purse, use two pieces of heavy adhesive stiffener (designed for curtain pelmets) between the wadding and the bandana fabric. Cut the pieces using the basic pattern shape, then trim ⅜in (1cm) all the way around before fixing it to the outer fabric with an iron, following the manufacturer's instructions.

Template
Photocopy at 200%

Needle case

A needle case is ideal for keeping sewing, embroidery and darning needles safe, particularly when travelling. This simple one has four linen 'pages' for needles and a magnet set in the centre of the front cover to corral them while you work.

1 Cut a strip of bandana measuring 4¾ x 18in (12 x 46cm). Cut the wadding and fusible interfacing into two 4in (10cm) squares. Fuse each wadding square to a square of fusible interfacing with an iron. Cut the stiffener into two equal squares measuring 4 x 3⅞in (10 x 9.5cm) and one narrow strip measuring 4 x ¼in (10cm x 5mm). Lay the bandana piece down in front of you wrong side up. Fuse the narrow strip of stiffener to it with an iron, positioning it exactly on the centre of the fabric with equal spaces above and below it. Then fuse the two pieces of cotton wadding on either side, leaving a ¼in (5mm) gap between them and the thin strip.

2 Turn your work over. Fold each side in along the edges of the cotton wadding and press. Now fold the two raw short edges at the centre back on themselves by ¼in (5mm) and press. Lay the herringbone tape down the centre, aligning the top and bottom edges with the fabric and covering the folded edges. Pin or tack along the top edge to hold everything in position.

SUPPLIES

- One bandana, minimum dimensions 18in (46cm) square, or fabric of your choice cut to those measurements
- 8 x 4in (20 x 10cm) of fusible interfacing
- 8 x 4in (20 x 10cm) of cotton wadding
- 8 x 4in (20 x 10cm) of heavyweight iron-on stiffener
- Six buttons ⅜in (1cm) in diameter or smaller
- Three pieces of 8 x 3½in (20 x 9cm) white linen
- 4¾in (12cm) of 1in (2.5cm)-wide white herringbone tape
- Circular adhesive magnets ⅜in (1cm) in diameter for fastening (optional)
- Scissors
- Iron
- Sewing machine
- Needle and pins
- Threads to match the fabrics
- Pinking shears

TIP
You can add adhesive magnets to the centre of the two pieces of stiffener before Step 5. Make sure they are not attached to the 'glue' side.

3 Pin or tack the bottom edges and the bottom end of the herringbone tape. Stitch ⅜in (1cm) seams along the top and bottom edges, reverse stitching at the beginning and ends of both seams. Trim the four corners close to, but not cutting, the stitching at 45 degrees. Do the same with the ends of the herringbone tape to reduce bulk.

4 Working through the gaps underneath the tape, turn your work right side out and flip the tape to the other side so that it lies underneath the two folded edges. Use a pin to ease the corners out and make them nice and sharp.

5 Press with a hot iron. Slip the two pieces of stiffener into the two pockets with the 4in (10cm) measurement lying vertically. Make sure that the 'glue' sides are facing as you do so.

6 With the stiffener pushed firmly into the corners of their pockets, fuse to the fabric with a hot iron. Tack down the folded edges where they overlap the tape, thus enclosing the stiffener, and topstitch by machine very close to the edge.

7 Trim the edges of the linen pieces with pinking shears. Fold them in half and press to find the centre. Open them out again and lay on your main piece with the crease lying down the middle of the herringbone tape. Anchor the linen to the outer with pairs of buttons — one on the inside and one on the outside — sandwiching all the layers of fabric and tape in between.

Flag

Celebrate summer, spring, holidays, birthdays, anniversaries, or even just lunch! Just like bunting, a flag makes any occasion special. This flag can be made in any simple or complicated assortment of colours – keep it fairly plain with just two colours, or use up all your scraps from other projects.

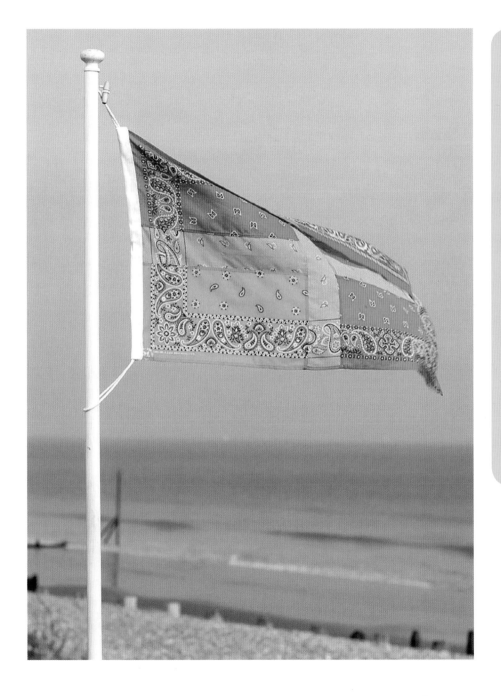

SUPPLIES

- Three bandanas, a minimum of 18in (46cm) square, or fabrics of your choice cut to this measurement, two in matching or similar colours and one in a contrasting colour
- 36in (91.5cm) of 1in (2.5cm)-wide white herringbone tape
- 42in (106cm) of piping cord
- 1¼in (3cm) wooden toggle
- White thread and thread to match main colours of the bandanas
- Pencil or air-erasable pen
- Ruler
- Measuring tape
- Scissors
- Sewing needle and pins
- Sewing machine
- Iron

PREPARING THE PATTERN PIECES

Cut four pieces of bandana 13¾ x 8¾in (35 x 22cm) for the four corner rectangles (see A on diagram). These need to be the same, or similar, colours. Cut two pieces 13¾ x 4in (35 x 10cm) (B), and one piece 17½ x 4in (44.5 x 10cm) (C) for the cross. These need to be in a contrasting colour to the rectangles. Lay the pieces out in their correct positions to one side so that you don't confuse the fabric sections when you are piecing them together.

1 Take the top left-hand A piece and pin or tack its long edge to the long edge of the left-hand B piece with wrong sides together. Machine-stitch a ⅜in (1cm) seam. Trim the seam edge of piece A down to half its depth.

2 Press the seam towards piece A, tucking under the overhang of piece B, encasing the raw edge of piece A and forming a clean flat fell seam (see page 42). Topstitch ⅛in (3mm) from the folded edge.

3 Repeat this process to attach the bottom left-hand panel. Do the same with the three right-hand pieces.

4 Attach both of these to the central piece C using the same type of enclosed hems.

TIP
Make a flagpole using 1⅜in (3.5cm)-diameter wooden dowelling topped off with a 1⅜in (3.5cm) wooden door handle, screwed on through its centre and reinforced with some glue.

5 Hem three sides of the flag, leaving one short end raw. Use an iron to fold the three edges ¼in (5mm) over, then ¼in (5mm) again. Stitch ⅛in (3mm) from the edge. Change the thread for each colour.

6 Fold one end of the piping cord 6in (15cm) from one end and use a zigzag stitch to secure the raw end in place. Tie the toggle 4¾in (12cm) from the other end of the piping cord and secure the raw end with zigzag stitch.

7 Lay the unhemmed edge of the flag along the herringbone tape, aligning it with the centre of the tape's width. Tack the flag edge to the centre of the tape. Fold in both ends of the tape about 1½in (4cm) to encase the corners of the flag at the top and bottom and pin or tack them in place. Lay the piping cord along the centre of the tape so that the toggle protrudes at the top, and the loop at the bottom.

8 Fold the tape in half lengthways, press, and pin or tack it to hold it in position, ensuring that the edges of the tape are aligned on either side of the flag. Make sure that the piping cord runs freely in the channel created by the tape, apart from where it is attached near the top. Stitch ⅛in (3mm) from the edge, reversing the stitching at both ends for strength.

Covered coat hanger

These lovely padded coat hangers are kind to your clothes, with the benefit of being 'non-slip' for finer garments. A nice touch for a guest room or a thoughtful present, this is a quick project with very satisfying results – you won't stop at making one.

1 Wrap the strip of wadding around the hanger, overlapping it as you go. Stitch the end down by hand to anchor it, or use a staple gun to attach the wadding at the end of each arm of the hanger.

2 Cut two pieces of bandana 15 x 5in (38 x 13cm). Place the two pieces of fabric right sides together and pin or tack along one short edge before machine stitching a ⅜in (1cm) seam. Press the seam open with a hot iron.

SUPPLIES
For each coat hanger:
- One bandana, a minimum of 18in (46cm) square, or fabric of your choice cut to this measurement
- 4in (10cm) square scrap of bandana
- 70 x 1½in (180 x 4cm) of cotton wadding (this can be made out of several strips sewn together by hand)
- One small button
- Staple gun (optional)
- Scissors
- Sewing needle, thread and pins
- Sewing machine
- Iron
- Embroidery thread to match (or contrast) with your fabric
- Embroidery needle
- Yo-yo maker (optional)

TIP
All instructions are to fit a standard simple 16½in (42cm)-wide crescent-shaped wooden coat hanger.

3 Turn the fabric over (now right side up and lying horizontally in front of you), fold the long bottom edge up to meet the top edge, and pin around the three raw edges.

4 Rounding off the corners, stitch a ⅜in (1cm) seam by machine, starting at the centre top (reverse stitching here for strength) and around one end, to meet the fold on the bottom edge. Stitch a similar seam on the other end, but this time starting 4in (10cm) from the end, thus leaving a large turning gap of roughly 9in (23cm) along one side of the top edge.

5 Turn right side out through the turning gap. Turn in the raw edges of the gap by ⅜in (1cm), press, and tack around the opening. At this point you may want to check whether the opening is big enough to slot your hanger into.

6 Starting at the top centre, working away from the turning gap and using your embroidery thread, sew running stitches by hand approximately ⅛in (3mm) around the fabric until you reach the other side of the turning gap. With the needle and thread still attached, feed your coat hanger into the fabric 'tube'. Pull your embroidery thread and tease the fabric so that it is gathered evenly across the width of the hanger.

7 With the two tacked and folded edges held together, carry on with your running stitch to close the turning gap. Finish the embroidery thread off with a few tight, small stitches.

8 Make 1¾in (4.5cm) yo-yos to stitch onto your padded coat hanger. You can use a yo-yo maker, in which case simply follow the manufacturer's instructions, or follow the instructions on page 48.

Wreath

An all-seasons decoration for outside or inside,
this wreath uses up all your little scraps of bandana fabric.
Make one in tones and shades of a single colour, or mix
complementary colours for vibrancy. This is a very simple,
quick project that does not involve any sewing.

SUPPLIES
To make a wreath roughly 16in (40cm) in diameter (although you can make this project any size you like):
• Scraps of bandanas (and plain cotton scraps to make up any deficit), or other fabric scraps of your choice
• 12in (30cm) embroidery hoop

1 The smallest of fabric pieces can be used to make this wreath, so whenever you make a project, always keep your scraps of fabric – I keep mine in an old galvanized bucket. Before you start, tip all your scraps onto your worktable and play around grouping them – contrasting colours, brights and monochromes – then decide which scraps you are going to use.

TIP
Lay the scraps out in a large circle and play around with the order of the colours before you start tying them on. This is a project that can be kept in progress, as you complete other projects and accumulate scraps.

2 Take the embroidery hoop apart and put the part with the screw fixing to one side. Don't waste it, though; you can use it to make another wreath – just tighten the screw and cover it with fabric as you tie the scraps on at Step 3. Paint the embroidery hoop with acrylic paint if you want to. One coat is probably enough as you will aim to cover it with fabric.

3 Cut any larger scraps down to size – the pieces should be an average of 6in (15cm) long, and no more than 1½in (4cm) wide, but their actual shape is not important, nor their raw edges. Tie the scraps around your wooden circle, taking time to make sure you are happy with the positions of the different colours and tones.

TIP
Think about accessorizing your wreath, perhaps with seasonal extras such as twigs and pine cones in the autumn, shells in the summer, baubles at Christmas, and leaves and blossoms in the spring. Tie on found objects from all seasons to create, over time, a wreath full of memories.

4 Continue tying on scraps until the hoop is completely covered. Over time, if left outside, the cotton fabric scraps will weather in the sun and fray in the wind, adding beautiful character to your wreath.

Nightdress case

This simple nightdress or lingerie case slips neatly under your pillow, is useful for travelling or to keep laundry separate in your suitcase. Resize the depth to 12in (30cm) plus a 6in (15cm) flap if you want to make a bigger one to fit pyjamas by using two bandanas.

1 Cut off the bandana's seams but keep these scraps for binding the sides of your case later. Press the bandana with a hot iron. Trim the bandana, interfacing and lining to 13¾ x 19in (35 x 48.5cm) and use the iron to fuse the interfacing to the wrong side of the bandana. With the bandana right side up, lay the lining fabric on top of it and align all the raw edges.

2 Pin or tack along the two short ends and stitch a ⅜in (1cm) seam.

SUPPLIES

- One bandana, minimum measurement 22in (56cm) square, or fabric of your choice cut to those measurements
- 15 x 21½in (38 x 55cm) of white cotton or linen for lining
- 15 x 21½in (38 x 55cm) of fusible interfacing
- Three small buttons
- One Dorset button, ¾in (2cm) in diameter (see page 47 for making instructions)
- White crochet thread or cotton embroidery thread
- Scissors
- Iron
- Sewing needles and pins
- White cotton thread
- Thread to match your bandana (just a small amount for attaching the buttons and topstitching)
- Sewing machine

3 Turn right side out and tease the two seams so that the edges are sharp before pressing them. Pin or tack along these edges and topstitch ⅛in (3mm) from the pressed edges. I worked from the bandana side and used white thread in the bobbin, with a thread matching the bandana on top.

4 With your work wrong side up and lying vertically in front of you, fold the bottom edge up 7½in (19cm), press it, and pin or tack in position. Cut two strips from the bandana scraps to measure 1½ x 14¼in (4 x 36cm) for binding the two sides of your case. Lay your work bandana side up, and pin one of the long strips along one of the long raw edges, right sides together. Position it so that it extends about ⅜in (1cm) at either end, trimming it if necessary. Pin or tack in position.

5 Stitch a ⅜in (1cm) seam along this edge. Fold up the binding to cover the seam selvedge and press. Turn your work over, fold the top edge of the binding strip down to meet the raw edge of the seam, and press. Finally, fold the binding down again to meet the stitch line of the seam and pin or tack in position.

6 Folding the extra binding in at either end, sew the binding down by hand with a small overstitch.

7 Make the ¾in (2cm)-diameter Dorset button (see page 47). You can leave it plain, or embroider on it to mimic the motifs in the bandana, or maybe 'half-make' its centre so that it resembles a wagon wheel. Folding the flap of your case down 4½in (11.5cm), decide upon the position of the button and stitch it on so that it sits ¾in (2cm) below the edge of the folded-down flap. Sew on the button.

8 To reduce the chance of the fabric tearing around the button, you can reinforce it by sewing a very small button onto the inside of the case, sandwiching the fabrics in between. Stitch two small buttons at the top left- and right-hand corners of the pocket to reinforce the stress point.

9 Make a button loop (see page 46) to correspond with the Dorset buttons, either in white or to match the colour of your bandana.

Shoe bags

These are useful, simple bags for storing shoes, whether stashing them away when they're out of season, popping in a suitcase or keeping them in pairs at the bottom of your wardrobe. The size shown is designed for a pair of women's flat-heeled shoes.

SUPPLIES
- One bandana, at least 20in (50cm) square, or fabric of your choice cut to those measurements
- 17 x 14in (43 x 35.5cm) of white cotton or linen for lining
- 28in (70cm) of ⅜in (1cm)-wide white herringbone tape for drawstring
- One small button
- Scissors
- Sewing needles and pins
- White cotton thread
- Sewing machine
- Iron
- Safety pin
- Thread to match your bandana (just a small amount for attaching the button)
- Sewing machine

TIP
To make bags for bulky shoes, first wrap them with paper and then use the size of the paper as your pattern. Add 6½in (16cm) to the width and 13in (33cm) to the length. Make the outer fabric 7in (18cm) longer than the lining fabric. For much larger bags, piece more than one bandana together.

1 Trim the bandana so that it measures 20in (50cm) square. Lay the lining fabric down vertically in front of you. Lay the bandana right side down on top of it and align all the raw edges. Pin or tack along the top edge and stitch a ⅜in (1cm) seam.

2 Press the seam towards the lining side. With the fabric laid out right side up and horizontally in front of you, fold the bottom long edge up to meet the top long edge. Carefully pin or tack all the way along this top edge, making sure that the seam is well aligned. Mark a ¾in (2cm) gap for the drawstring, starting 5½in (14cm) before and finishing 6in (15cm) before the bandana meets the lining. Stitch a ⅜in (1cm) seam along this long edge.

3 Press the long seam open. Turn open the raw edges of the selvedge around the opening gap and stitch down by hand to reduce fraying.

4 With your long tube of fabric still inside out, press it flat so that the long seam lies centrally along its length. Align the fabric at the lining end and pin or tack. Stitch a ⅜in (1cm) seam along the edge, leaving a 5in (13cm) turning gap. Trim the two corners at 45 degrees to make them nice and sharp when you turn the bag out.

5 Align the fabric at the bandana end and pin or tack. Stitch a ⅜in (1cm) seam along this edge. If it is fairly fine fabric it is not necessary to trim the corners at 45 degrees.

6 Pull your bag right side out gently through the turning gap.

7 At the lining end, fold in the raw edges of the turning gap by ⅜in (1cm) and pin. Close the turning gap by hand with small, neat overstitches.

8 Push the bandana outer down inside the lining so that the corners meet snugly. In doing so, the bandana fabric folds over to line the top 3¼in (8cm) of your bag. Check on the bandana side that the drawstring gap is positioned just below the bandana/lining seam. Press with a hot iron and pin or tack along the seam joining the two fabrics. Sew two lines of stitching, one just below the seam on the lining, and the other ⅝in (1.5cm) below it to create a channel for the drawstring. Finish the thread ends off neatly by hand.

9 Take the length of herringbone tape and feed it through the drawstring channel using a safety pin.

10 Fold both ends of the tape over by ¼in (5mm) and then ¼in (5mm) again. Stitch them down securely by hand. Make sure that the protruding herringbone-tape tail ends are the same length. Find the centre of the back of your bag and stitch a small button through both layers of fabric and the tape to anchor it firmly in place – this will prevent the tape ends from disappearing into the channel in the future.

Materials, Equipment and Techniques

A sewing machine (see page opposite) is essential for making the projects in this book. You will also need a steam iron and ironing board on hand to press your work as you go.

Other items you will need include: cotton bandanas ❶, piping cord ❷, cord elastic ❸, pencil ❹, air-erasable pen ❺, threads ❻, toggles ❼, purse frame ❽, buttons ❾, measuring tape ❿, self-cover buttons ⓫, ruler ⓬, herringbone tapes ⓭, embroidery threads ⓮, wooden bag handles ⓯,

embroidery hoop ⓰, sewing needles ⓱, pins ⓲, small brass curtain rings ⓳, yo-yo maker ⓴, bias binding ㉑, scissors ㉒, insulated wadding ㉓, fusible interfacing ㉔, cotton wadding ㉕, iron-on stiffener ㉖ and sewing machine zipper foot.

WORKING WITH FABRIC

Choosing fabric

Select natural fibres whenever possible: linens, cottons or linen/cotton mixes. Natural fibres are best washed before use to pre-shrink them. Choose good-quality stiffeners and interfacings. I always use natural cotton wadding.

For trims and ties, use traditional rickrack, piping cord, herringbone and woven tapes, 100% cotton threads and plain buttons – cover your own or make Dorset buttons (see page 47).

Pattern placement

If you are using a printed bandana for your project, it is worth spending time planning the placement of the design when cutting your fabric. The best way to do this is to cut a 'window' template. Cut your template shape out of the middle of a piece of paper and move it about over the fabric to choose the pattern section you like.

Measuring

A measuring tape can be substituted with a ruler. Make sure you consistently use either imperial or metric measurements and do not mix the two.

Marking

Use an air-erasable pen or a fabric marker. Most fade after a couple of hours, but do check as some need washing out. Tailor's chalk can be brushed away. Use white chalk on dark cloth and coloured chalk on lighter fabrics. The chalk should be kept sharp to produce a clean line. If your design is going to be stitched with a dark thread, you can simply use a very fine, sharp pencil to mark the fabric.

Cutting

Ideally, you should have two pairs of sewing scissors. A small pair of sharp, pointed scissors is essential for cutting threads and trimming corners and curves. Sewing shears have long blades and a bent handle so that the scissors can rest on the table while cutting, keeping the fabric flat. Make sure your shears are used solely for fabrics and keep them sharp – it is a good idea to get them sharpened every couple of years.

Pinning and tacking (basting)

Pinning and tacking seams before you sew ensures that the fabric will not slip about when stitching, thereby producing a straight, neat seam. Pins with coloured glass heads are easy to find in fabric. Place your pins at right angles to your stitching line if you want to machine stitch over them and avoid having to tack or baste.

Tacking, also known as basting, is a temporary stitch used to fix pieces of fabric in position ready for permanent stitching. It is the easiest and quickest hand-sewing stitch. Knot the end of the thread and work large running stitches about ⅜in (1cm) long **A**. Finish with a couple of stitches worked over each other to secure the end. When the seam or hem has been permanently sewn by machine, remove the tacking.

USING A SEWING MACHINE

Keep your sewing machine regularly serviced and covered when not in use. Always refer to your instruction booklet for information on threading, changing stitches, reversing and so on. Set up your machine somewhere with plenty of light and where you can sit at the machine comfortably.

Make sure that the machine is threaded correctly and that the threads from the needle and bobbin are placed away from you towards the back of the machine. Turn the wheel towards you so that the needle is in the work. Taking it slowly will help you control the machine and make problems with tension or tangling threads less likely.

Two-colour sewing

I regularly sew with one colour threaded on the machine needle and a different colour in the bobbin below. This is useful when sewing together two different-coloured fabrics, making the stitching less visible on both sides. I keep little pill boxes of fully charged bobbins in all the colours I'll be using in projects **A**, so that I can swap the bobbin over quickly when I need to.

When using this technique it is especially important that your stitch tension is even so that the alternative colours are not pulled through to be visible on the other side of your fabric.

BASIC STITCHES

I don't go in for fancy sewing-machine stitching: the basics of straight stitching, zigzag stitching, topstitching and reverse stitching are all you need to make the projects in this booklet.

Straight stitch

Used for all flat seams, hems and topstitching. You can alter the length of straight stitch – at its longest it can be used for gathering or tacking (basting).

Topstitching

A line of straight machine stitching worked on the right side of the fabric, parallel to seams and edges. It can be used as both a decorative and a functional stitch, providing extra strength to a hem or seam.

Zigzag stitch

Used along raw edges to help reduce fraying. Zigzag stitches can also be used decoratively or to strengthen pressure or stress points. You can alter the length of the stitches and how close together they are. When changing from straight stitch to zigzag (or vice versa) without breaking your stitching, always adjust your stitch function with the foot down (to hold your fabric in position) and the needle up.

Reverse stitching

This reinforces or strengthens the beginning and end of a line of stitching, particularly in areas where pressure or stress will occur. It can also be used as a quick way to start and end stitching without having to finish off thread ends by hand.

BASIC SEAMS

Flat seams

Place two pieces of fabric together, right sides facing, then pin or tack. Machine stitch ⅜in (1cm) from, and parallel to, the raw edges of the fabric. Finish the beginning and end of your line of stitching by reverse stitching.

Finishing off threads

Finish off thread ends by threading them onto a sewing needle and making a couple of small, tight stitches before cutting the thread off.

Trimming corners and curves

Corners should be trimmed to an angle of 90 degrees so they are sharp when the work is turned right side out. On curved seams, cut V-shapes close to the stitch line. This will allow the seam to be smooth when the work is turned right side out.

Pressing seams

Have all the equipment for ironing set up before you start a project. Press each seam as you complete it. Use the point of the iron to open seams, then steam press for a crisp edge and a flat seam.

Unpicking seams

A seam ripper (or stitch unpicker) is a useful tool for unpicking stitches. Insert the pointed blade underneath the thread to be cut. Push it forwards against the thread and the blade will cut it. It is possible to run the blade along a line of stitching between the two layers of fabric and cut all the stitches in one movement, but this requires some skill to avoid cutting the fabric.

FLAT FELL SEAM

A flat fell seam is most commonly used on tailored shirts or the inside leg seam of jeans. It has one or two lines of visible stitching and no raw edges showing on either side. This seam is equally finished and neat on both sides and therefore perfect for use on reversible projects.

1 To create a flat fell seam on the garment inside, stitch a ⅜in (1cm) seam with your fabrics wrong sides together.

2 With the seam lying horizontal in front of you, press the seam away from you. Trim the front seam allowance to ⅛in (3mm) from the seam stitching.

3 Fold the longer seam allowance over the trimmed portion and press in place. It is important that the fold width remains consistent along the seam. Press the whole of the folded seam allowance down towards you and pin or tack in position.

4 Topstitch close to the folded edge to enclose the raw edges.

> **TIP**
> These seams can be fiddly to do at first. Be careful not to scorch your fingers at Step 3.

BINDING EDGES

Use tape, bias binding or strips of fabric to bind raw edges. If you are making your own binding from strips of fabric, cut them wider than needed, fold the long edges in and press them before starting.

1 Cut the binding to the required length plus at least ¾in (2cm). Lay it along the edge of the work so that the middle lies exactly over the raw fabric edge. Pin or tack in position and topstitch along the binding ⅛in (3mm) or less from the edge. If binding all the way around a piece of work, join it by folding the end under ⅜in (1cm), overlapping the beginning of the binding and stitching along this fold.

2 Turn the work over. Fold the tape down to meet the stitch line and encase the raw edges. Hem by hand by overstitching.

MAKING BOX CORNERS

1 Place the two pieces of fabric right sides together. Using a straight stitch, and the indicated seam allowance, sew the side and bottom seams. Pivot at the corners by leaving the needle down, raising the foot and turning the fabric 90 degrees.

2 Press the seams open. With the sewn fabric still right sides together, match the side seam with the bottom fold (or seam) to create a point at the corner. Pin to hold them together. It is very important to match the seams exactly; this will make the finished corner look good.

3 Mark the line of the box corner with a pencil so the depth is measured from side to side at the base of the point. This boxed corner depth is 4in (10cm), measured from the tip of the corner.

4 Sew across the point on the drawn line several times, reverse stitching at the beginning and end for extra strength.

5 Trim away the peak to ¼in (5mm) from the line.

HAND STITCHES

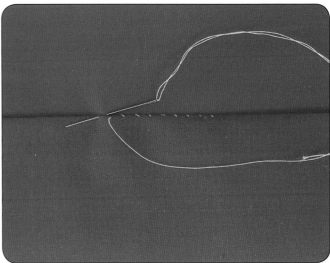

Overstitch

Use overstitch for closing the openings left for turning. With your two pieces of fabric pinned or tacked together, bring your needle up from within one folded edge to the front of your work. Now push the needle diagonally through both folded layers, catching a few threads of fabric from each. Pull the needle and thread through and repeat, spacing the stitches between ⅛in (3mm) and ¼in (5mm) apart.

Hem stitch

Similar to overstitch, this stitch is used for hand stitching hems.

> **TIP**
> Run the needle along the inside of the fabric fold between stitches to keep the work almost invisible.

Blanket stitch

1 Imagine two parallel stitch lines roughly ¼in (5mm) apart. Bring your thread through to the front of your work on the left-hand line. Insert the needle in position ¼in (5mm) further along in the right-hand line and through to the front again parallel to where it was inserted, at the same time keeping the working thread under the needle point (1a). Pull your thread through and to the left to form an L-shape (1b).

2 Reinsert the needle ¼in (5mm) further along in the right-hand line and through to the front again parallel to where it was inserted before, at the same time keeping the working thread under the needle point. Continue, creating an even line of stitches.

Backstitch

1 Bring the thread through to the front of your fabric on your stitch line. Make a small running stitch, about ¼in (5mm) long, along the stitch line, bringing the needle back through to the front again, ¼in (5mm) from your first stitch.

2 Reinsert the needle ¼in (5mm) back along the stitch line at the point where your last stitch went through to the back of your work. Pull the needle through to the front again, ¼in (5mm) ahead of the last stitch. Continue, creating a solid line of ¼in (5mm) stitches.

BUTTON LOOPS

1 Sew on the button. Use pins to mark the position of the loop. Push the threaded needle up through the fabric's folded edge at the point of the left-hand pin, leaving the knotted end within the fold. Push the needle back in again at the point of the right-hand pin and out again by the left-hand pin. Pull the needle to leave a loop of thread wide enough to go over the button. Repeat stitching through at the two marker pins until the loop has four strands.

2 Remove the two marker pins. Starting at the right-hand side, sew small buttonhole stitches (tight blanket stitches) over all the strands and the loose thread until you reach the left-hand side. Fasten off securely with a few small, tight stitches.

3 The button should fit neatly into the loop.

TIP
Button loops are much easier to make for small buttons than traditional buttonholes and are very satisfying to sew.

DORSET BUTTONS

This style of button dates back to 1600. They add beautiful character to any hand-stitched project. It takes some practice to get the crossing of the 'spokes' central, so don't worry if your wheel is off-centre – this can be excused as handmade charm.

1 Thread an embroidery needle with thread. Tie one end of the thread onto the curtain ring. Work in blanket stitch around the circumference of the ring, covering the raw knot end with the first few stitches.

2 Make sure you make enough stitches to cover the ring completely. Stitch into the first stitch again to hide the join. Slide the stitches around the ring so that the outside blanket stitch ridge is now on the inside of the ring and the outside edge is smooth.

3 Wrap your thread around the ring from top to bottom. Turn the ring slightly and wrap the thread around again. Continue until you have wrapped ten times to create the spokes of the wheel. At this point the threads will look somewhat random; use the end of your needle to tweak and reposition them so they are dispersed evenly around the ring. Make a couple of stitches in the centre of the wheel to secure the spokes and even them out.

> **TIP**
> Use different-coloured threads in steps 2, 3 and 4 to create interesting new designs for your buttons.

4 Using backstitch, work your way around the spokes in a clockwise spiral from the centre outwards. Thread ends can be finished off, but leave one or two of them long to fix your button to the fabric.

MAKING A YO-YO

A yo-yo is used to embellish the Covered Coat Hanger (see page 26). If you have a yo-yo maker, simply follow the manufacturer's instructions. Otherwise follow the instructions below.

1 Cut a circle of fabric 4in (10cm) in diameter. With the wrong side facing you, fold the edges in by ¼in (5mm) and press with a hot iron. Then bring the needle through from the back and make ¼in (5mm) gathering stitches (like stitching a hem), all around the edge with your thread doubled for strength.

2 Draw your thread to gather in the folded edge to the centre.

3 Push the needle through the centre to the back and make a few small stitches to finish off the thread and firmly secure the gathering.

TIP
These embellishments are perfect for using up scraps to decorate projects or make sweet little corsages with a button or a bead in the centre.

4 When complete, stitch the yo-yo onto the project you have made. You can use a small button to anchor the yo-yo into position.